OSSUARIES

POETRY BY DIONNE BRAND

'Fore Day Morning (1978)

Earth Magic (for children 1980/1993/2006)

Winter Epigrams and Epigrams to Ernesto Cardenal in Defense of Claudia (1983)

Primitive Offensive (1983)

Chronicles of the Hostile Sun (1984)

No Language Is Neutral (1990)

Land to Light On (1997)

thirsty (2002)

Inventory (2006)

Ossuaries (2010)

OSSUARIES

DIONNE BRAND

McClelland & Stewart

LIBRARY AND ARCHIVES CANADA CATALOGUING IN PUBLICATION

Brand, Dionne
Ossuaries / Dionne Brand.

Poems.
ISBN 978-0-7710-1734-6

I. Title.

PS8553.R275087 2010   C811'.54   C2009-905156-7

Published simultaneously in the United States of America by McClelland & Stewart Ltd., P.O. Box 1030, Plattsburgh, New York 12901

Library of Congress Control Number: 2009935660

We acknowledge the financial support of the Government of Canada through the Book Publishing Industry Development Program and that of the Government of Ontario through the Ontario Media Development Corporation's Ontario Book Initiative. We further acknowledge the support of the Canada Council for the Arts and the Ontario Arts Council for our publishing program.

Typeset in Golden Cockerel by M&S, Toronto
Printed and bound in Canada

ANCIENT FOREST
FRIENDLY

This book is printed on acid-free paper that is 100% recycled, ancient-forest friendly (100% post-consumer waste).

McClelland & Stewart Ltd.
75 Sherbourne Street
Toronto, Ontario
M5A 2P9
www.mcclelland.com

1   2   3   4   5   14   13   12   11   10

For Constance Rooke

...you could emerge from car wrecks
as elegantly as from weddings...

OSSUARIES

ossuary I

I lived and loved, some might say,
in momentous times,
looking back, my dreams were full of prisons

in our narcotic drifting slumbers,
so many dreams of course were full of prisons,
mine were without relief

in our induced days and our wingless days,
my every waking was incarcerated,
each square metre of air so toxic with violence

the atmospheres were breathless there,
the bronchial trees were ligatured
with carbons

some damage I had expected, but no one
expects the violence of glances, of offices,
of walkways and train stations, of bathroom mirrors

especially, the vicious telephones, the coarseness of
daylight, the brusque decisions of air,
the casual homicides of dresses

what brutal hours, what brutal days,
do not say, oh find the good in it, do not say,
there was virtue; there was no virtue, not even in me

let us begin from there, restraining metals
covered my heart, rivulets
of some unknown substance transfused my veins

at night, especially at night, it is always at night,
a wall of concrete enclosed me,
it was impossible to open my eyes

I lived like this as I said without care,
tanks rolled into my life, grenades took root
in my uterus, I was sickly each morning, so dearly

what to say,
life went on around me,
I laughed, I had drinks, I gathered with friends

we grinned our aluminum teeth,
we exhaled our venomous breaths,
we tried to be calm in the invisible architecture

we incubated, like cluster bombs,
whole lives waiting, whole stellar regions,
discoveries of nebulae, and compassion

from the cities the electric rains pierced us,
the ceaseless bitter days folded like good linen,
the phosphorous streets gave off their harmful lights

we bit our fingernails to blue buttons,
we staggered at the high approach of doorways,
plunged repeatedly to our deaths only to be revived

by zoos, parades, experiments, exhibits, television sets,
oh we wanted to leave, we wanted to leave
the aspirated syllables and villages, the skeletal

dance floors, the vacant, vacant moons that tortured us,
when the jailers went home and the spectators drifted
away and the scientists finished their work

like a bad dog chained to an empty gas station,
for blue blue nights,
I got worse and worse, so troubling

I would fall dead like a specimen,
at the anthropometric spectacles
on the Champ de Mars, the Jardin d'Acclimatation

the mobile addresses of the autopsy fields,
though I could see no roads,
I was paid for losing everything, even eyesight

I lived in the eternal villages, I lived like a doll,
a shaggy doll with a beak, a bell, a red mouth,
I thought, this was the way people lived, I lived

I had nights of insentient adjectives,
shale nights, pebbled nights, stone nights,
igneous nights, of these nights, the speechlessness

I recall, the right ribs of the lit moon,
the left hip of the lit moon,
what is your name they asked, I said nothing

I heard the conspiratorial water,
I heard the only stone, I ate her shoulder,
I could not hear myself, you are mistaken I said to no one

the chain-link fences glittered like jewellery,
expensive jewellery, portable jewellery,
I lost verbs, whole, like the hull of almonds

after consideration you will discover, as I,
that verbs are a tragedy, a bleeding cliffside, explosions,
I'm better off without, with vermillion, candles

this bedding, this mercy,
this stretcher, this solitary perfectable strangeness,
and edge, such cloth this compass

of mine, of earth, of mourners of these
reasons, of which fairgrounds, of which theories
of plurals, of specimens of least and most, and most

of expeditions,
then travels and wonders then journeys,
then photographs and photographs of course

the multiplications of which, the enormity of this,
and drill-bits and hammers and again handcuffs,
and again rope, coarse business but there

some investigations, then again the calculations,
such hours, such expansions, the mind dizzy
with leaps, such handles, of wood, of thought

and then science, all science, all murder,
melancholic skulls, pliant to each fingertip,
these chromatic scales, these calipers the needle

in the tongue, the eyes' eye, so
whole diameters, circumferences, locutions,
an orgy of measurements, a festival of inches

gardens and paraphernalia of measurements,
unificatory data, curious data,
beautiful and sensuous data, oh yes beautiful

now, of attractions and spectacles of other sheer forces,
and types in the universe, the necessary
exotic measurements, rarest, rarest measuring tapes

a sudden unificatory nakedness, bificatory nakedness,
of numbers, of violent fantasms
at exhibitions again, of walks, of promenades

at fairs with products, new widgets, human widgets,
with music, oh wonders,
the implications

then early in this life, like mountains,
already pictures and pictures, before pictures,
after pictures and cameras

their sickness, eye sickness, eye murder,
murder sickness, hunger sickness,
this serendipity of calculators, of footprints

with fossils, their wingspan of all time,
at crepuscules' rare peace time, if only,
like water, in daytime, no solace, so, so different

from solitude, all solitude, all madness,
so furious, so numerous, the head, the markets,
the soles of the feet, so burnt, so thin

and the taste, so meagre, so light-headed,
the cloud flashes, the lightning geometry,
the core of reflectivity so vastly, vastly vast

the wait now, lumens of aches, such aches,
the horizontal and the vertical aches of lightning,
its acoustics, loud pianos, percussive yet

strings and quartets, multicellular runnels yet and yet,
the altitude of the passageway, its precipitation
and grand arithmetic, the segments

the latitudes of where, where and here,
its contours, its eccentric curvatures,
so presently, angular and nautical, all presently

just fine my lungs, just fine,
hypothesis absolutely, but just fine,
why lungs, strange theory

oh yes and the magnitude of jaundice, trenches,
like war, continuous areas and registers, logarithms
so unexplainable, rapid scales, high notes

besides, anyway so thermal, atmospheric,
wondrous aggressions, approximately here,
elaborate like radiation and seismic, yes all over

the bodies' symptoms of algebraic floods,
tiredness for one, weariness actually,
weary with magnetic embryos

petals, yes petals of sick balm please, now yes,
for my esophagus, analgesics of indigo,
of wires, of electric shocks, why eucalyptus leaves

of course lemon grass, labernum, please, lion's claw,
remedies of cloves, bitter bark,
still birdless though, worldless

asthma with blueness, then music,
gardens truthfully, truthfully nauseous with
tonsured numbers, volumes of fibres, embroidery

and hair nets of violence, blue,
like machine guns, of course knives, extensions
of blueness, all right then wherever

same radiations, lines in the forehead,
tapers, electrodes, invisible to the eyes,
official hammers and corkscrews, official grass

official cities now for appearances after all this,
all these appearances, generous, for certain
scraggly, wan, and robust appearances

assignments and hidden schedules of attendance,
a promise of blindness, a lover's clasp of
violent syntax and the beginning syllabi of verblessness

ossuary II

to undo, to undo and undo and undo this infinitive
of arrears, their fissile mornings,
their fragile, fragile symmetries of gain and loss

this is how she wakes each day of each underground year,
confessions late and half-hearted pour from her sleeping
mouth, beginning in the year of her disappearances

the grateful rooms had to be gathered into their temporal
shapes, the atmosphere coaxed to visible
molecules, definite arrangements of walls and doors

solidity lies beside her in its stigmatic shreds,
I, the slippery pronoun, the ambivalent, glistening,
long sheath of the alphabet flares beyond her reach

how then to verify her body, rejuvenate the blood-dead
arm, quell her treacherous stomach, its heaving solar
jumps, or seduce the preposition, where and where

her neck crackles to the radio voice, that coastal beacon,
last night she exchanged one set of keys for another,
her palms, branched, copper basins outstretched

now one numb finger, one thumb searched,
through all their known grammars for which
room, which dewy bed, and then what fateful day

nearsighted she needs her glasses yes, to summarize
the world, without them she's defenceless,
that's why they're always at the precipice of the bed

some violent drama was as usual surging,
on the airwaves and "plane" she heard, the usual
supercilious timbres hysterical, a cut larynx

she thought of splinters, slivering boards,
scooped the glasses from her abdomen to align
her brain, here notice, notice what is false from true

what is possible, and where's the doorway of this room,
kinetic news breaking sunlight,
but where was she, which city, what street

Albany, Buffalo, Havana, back tracks, Algiers,
to the swift boat ride from the south of Spain, back when,
the brief embossed room, a reversal, a body at sea

then, the short wave asserted, Manhattan,
Yasmine's tingling hand summoned the volume
in its circumference of black plastic, she

could not be in Manhattan, though the radio insisted,
her back alert like paintings to its usual ache,
some mornings she could return to sleep even

in the middle of the most gruesome news,
caught,
caught, every comrade caught

she could delay events with this groggy chemistry
of spasms and refusals,
a drowning, that second sleep, in lists of the undone

ungiven, unsought, the nausea could last days,
this room took shape now in yellow and brown,
a window lay behind a wilting curtain, tepid sunlight

the radio veered once again toward her, speeding,
"explosion," it mourned,
a kitchen knife, spanner, tweezers, skill saw

she felt a joy innocent like butter open her,
blinding stratus, ants, tongs, bolts, rust,
the whole ionosphere bounced into her mouth

glancing against her teeth, exceeding her nostrils, her
heart burrowed,
in corks, broken bottles, nails, finned incendiaries

she flew like shrapnel off the bed,
felt her way blind, as fire with slender strands,
as glaze, sand, starch caps, uniforms, and bracelets

the prepositions are irrelevant today, whichever house,
which century, wherever she was,
the bruised wires, severed, this they only ever dreamed

she would love, love to talk to them today,
though the dreaming had come to little and no end,
and less, there in the grey blood of the television

the spectacular buildings falling limpid, to nothing,
rims, aluminum, windowless, fragile staircases,
she wanted, wanted to whisper into telephones

it's done, someone had done it, someone,
had made up for all the failures,
she looked, pitiless, at the rubble, the shocked

the stumbling shattered dressed for work,
the powdering towers, the walls and windows
stuck to their skins like makeup and grease

look, the seared handbags, the cooked briefcases,
wheels, clocks, the staggered floors,
the startled one-winged orioles

the flights of starlings interrupted,
the genocides of September insects,
the disappearances after of sugar bees and quick footsteps

it was just past nine in any city,
but a glass of wine would do, a beer, a toke,
here's to the fatal future

how many times they'd asked each other,
you are ready to die but are you ready to kill,
she had been willing once

a jealousy orbiting her skull, its brittle calcium,
outside everywhere burned skin,
would she have flown into that willing skin

what equations she wondered of steel's pressure,
and concrete, matter and vacuum and terrible faith,
of sacred books, of tattooed foreheads, of small knives

she believed in nothing too, not broken hearts,
not blood with wine, not beloveds,
not the weight of her eyelids nor her own intentions

not even people whom she'd once admitted
were her hopes, and what she'd calculated
all her acts against

but failure is when they describe what you've done,
and she lives in that description hand to mouth,
outside the everyday, in refugee shafts

and tiny rooms, and in other people's passports,
in mathematical theorems of trust,
in her vigilant skin and feathery, feathery deceit

it is not enough to change the bourgeois state,
this sentence slumbered in her, sleek,
you have to bring it down, winched to this

each dawn's lurid ambivalence,
the chest fire flaring on any sofa, any chair, any bed,
the calculus of infidelity on each forehead kissed

she read the periodic table of elements in an eyebrow,
the length of patience in love,
this moment to depart in coffee's taste

fall crept now in the rind of deciduous stems,
and she could read it seconds before it arrived,
and hear birds and their music head south like musicians

packing up kit, decamping stale beer-smelling
halls, the floors' sly self-serving penitence,
the dismissive flutter of high-speed wings

it was sunny, a pale sunny, and the lindens down
three storeys spun their leaves tipped yellow,
grim joy overtook her

come the true fall here, come the fall, the romance
with the air is over but now,
now, who has such mortal imagination

her joy was not grim, her knuckles knotted in her lap,
insisted, yes she is aware that joy is grim, how these
two make a marriage, how long their courtship in her

house finches in the eavestroughs
went about their fall business, remorseless,
their urban quickness, their rapid knowledgeable song

and she had mourned enough for a thousand
broken towers, her eyesight washed immaculate and
caustic, her whole existence was mourning, so what?

ossuary III

I loved and lived, as I said, for a time,
looking up from water like sea shells,
I arrived where the sonorous oceans took me

washed and washed, coral overcame my feet, my hands,
the shocks of immobility, the stung tendons,
the clamped Achilles, the enamel vocal cords

I did well they say, given the circumstances,
the spiked municipalities rationed their handouts
of free breads, free bicycles, free bracelets

free sugars, free plastics, free razor blades,
free bullets, free coverings, free enclosures,
free fences, free, free, absolutely free freeness

still they required performances,
one needed licences and stamped forms, and masks,
and stickers and worse of all transparent veins

to be frank most of my time was spent
sleeping in one courthouse or another defending
charges of one thing and another

larcenies, robberies, trespassing,
loitering, intimidation, resisting arrest, vagrancy,
but fundamentally existence

I took my case everywhere, naturally,
all continents, several unknown galaxies, some as yet
unarmed moons, needless to say, nameless to count

the prodigious silence, the thunderclaps of
salutary ignorance,
so as I said momentous, ravenous, ugly times

I am aware how this looks, like pins
and fractile glass, and after a time anyone could see,
the futile jurisdictions and all my waterlogged paper

lived and loved, common oxymoron,
if I have lived, I have not loved,
and if I have loved, I cannot have lived

it was difficult to live and love at the same time,
you see what I mean,
since to live is to be rapacious as claws, to have

the most efficient knives and broken beer bottles,
needles, powers of attorney,
nonchalance, indifference, negligence

to love is an impediment to this hard business
of living
so I cannot have loved, not me

do not think this of me, do not think
I did not try to breach the fluorescent streets,
to admit the long-disillusioned sandbanks, do not think it

I rented secretive rooms to see what it was like,
no denying, I spread prickling sheets on narrowing beds,
stretched out beside one person and then another

the night dew we collected at our throats, cackling,
the cardamon aroma of our breaths, the cinnamon
we rubbed in our hands before touching

the basil leaves with which we covered ourselves,
obviously my rainy rainy eyes, my earth-filled hair,
all this I brought across sticky bitumen highways

to the dim-lit ambiguous approaches of these stanzas,
their permanences, their impermanences,
we wore in our heavy, heavy coats

the dried lavender flowers I crushed in my palms
before opening the doors,
my coastal limbs carrying shells and seaweeds

the full ocean in my mouth, oh I longed, longed
for the deepest suicidal blue waters, I craved the seas,
where what was on earth could not scar me

I gave all this to lovers, I gave them too my glasses,
we looked through windows from hotels off
freeways, off the industrial parks, off garbage dumps

we saw demolitions that stung our eyes rheumy,
indefinable liquids passed through our indefinable
souls

here I am then, goodbye, again and again,
how we left these rooms fully clothed twigs,
and branded bones again

do not say, do not say it was my fault,
do not say I could have gathered blue dragonflies,
or the showering sunlight

the ashes of volcanoes or the residue of songs
from the cups of saxophones
I could not, I could not, I could not

have raised ferned cadavers, thistles, tabebuia rosea,
anthurium horses,
could not, tribes of tigers and ginger lily

cartridges,
I tried love, I did,
the scapulae I kissed, I did

the flat triangular bones I filled with kisses, spumes
of kisses, gutters of kisses, postponed kisses,
and early new-born kisses

the curve of clavicles, I dug artesian wells of kisses there,
utensils of kisses,
spoons of kisses, basins of kisses, creeks of kisses

the jugular notch I ate in kisses,
I devoured in kisses,
teeth-filled kisses, throat-filled kisses, gullet-stuffed kisses

so don't tell me how love will rescue me,
I was carnivorous about love, I ate love to the ankles,
my thighs are gnawed with love

still and yet I cannot have loved,
since living was all I could do and for that,
I was caged in bone spur endlessly

eye sockets ambushed me,
I slept with harassment and provocations,
though I wanted to grow lilacs, who wouldn't?

to know the secrets of spiders, who wouldn't?
yet the rumours of newspapers persisted, the pained sighs
of the waiting rooms of existence were called good music

I could not leave my house without plans,
a perfect stranger's thought, and bone would sprout
on my heart like a lantern trapping a light

ossuary IV

oh heart, oh heart, blind like daylight,
when they came back, it was Albany and clear,
1977, from Algiers and Cairo and she's forgiven him

he had of course never asked for forgiveness, she
had not forgiven him publicly, not to his face,
that is she had not said, "I forgive you"

though a deep hatred like forgiveness erupted in her,
that year, that year, fractious like parchment,
she grew lavenders in small clay pots, read *The Origin*

of the Family and *The Eighteenth Brumaire*, "The tradition of all
dead generations weighs like a nightmare on the brains of
the living . . ." nursed the air of their small apartment

gave it patchouli incense, marijuana, eucalyptus oils,
the smoke of three thousand cigarettes, one after another,
the clatter of wooden beads around her neck and wrists

a front door painted red then black then red again,
she found her true mind drifting on the ceiling,
soaring away from him on the loosening tether of Engels

"You're nothing, Yas,
I made you something by fucking you,
other that that, you're nothing."

his motionless face, redundantly handsome, condescending,
as if this truth should give her comfort

comrades, speechless, as if
this rhetoric twirling from his tongue,
corkscrewed across the room

has struck them dumb like some edict,
outrageous and extravagant,
as if from a god

as if she should hear instead Monk's
"Crepuscule with Nellie," its deliberate
and loving notes scoring her back

Yasmine slips out the room, a volcanic mist,
molten through the doorframe,
brain on fire, "Give her a break, huh?"

finally finds a tongue "We got work to do." But
she's gone, a low hum, a bacteria, incubates in her left ear,
Charles Mingus recovers her, "Pithecanthropus

Erectus," and he does, then she was
three and her mother lifted the needle on the record,
the rushing out and out her feet tingling

bare on the pavement the day is finished,
her planet's already spun one millennia around the sun,
and the world as she knows it is vanished and

she's sitting on the unpolished floor of the boarding
house with her mother and the record player, and the true
meaning of things, run, run, as far as after yourself

she reads later that Mingus said the last movement
suggests the "frantic burst of a dying organism,"
and there with her mother, her feet bare on the floor

the planets already spun for months and years, she's
run out in 1977, past the loose hysterical trills of wood
winds, past the small ambitions meant for her

she looked then at the beacon of the record player,
to lead her out of the intuitions of gloom
and penury, but more, a science of incalculable waste

gleaming on every body in every boarding house they'd
lived, a glistening powder, an iridescent toxin,
whose only antibody was music and all she learned later

as early she knew she'd get up off that floor and walk,
right out beyond the broken parts, beyond her mother's
skirt, her brother's preacherly advice, his certain god

going over the realizations of Cairo, holding the faithful
in a future year in this Albany apartment,
Miles's "Bitches Brew" on the stereo and Fanon

like a double-edged knife in her teeth,
she's been wearing its ambivalent jewel like a tongue
ring, a gag it's true, it's true what Owusu said

"Pharoah's Dance" had been playing for thirteen
of its twenty minutes, Owusu lies on the floor digging
Miles, he loved Miles, the thin mean horn she hated

and Cairo, he called to her in the bathroom again,
about Cairo, the crossings of revolutionaries,
the bottle of sickly wine they drank was almost finished

the cynicism and who gives a fuck trumpet, that
should have been her first warning, now see,
the desert dust she'd missed seeing this December

when he opines, of their great mosques,
their cool stones, their great light signifying,
nothing between god and the human

she says maliciously who hefted the stone,
who carried the water, who fed the fires,
who opened the gates, who washed the clothes

who cut the wood, crushed the olives and palm into oils,
who bore the weight of all these gods,
whose eyes were put out to make their light

"when these people are in the world . . ." Engels ran
around her skull ". . . that will be the end of it . . ."
like water around the washed rim of a bowl

here's the difference, she told him,
between Miles and Bird,
Miles kept living, till life was rancid, Bird flew off

next dawn she paces the cobalt path,
from kitchen to living room, blue black,
living room to blue black kitchen until light

came through the blinds, light
as it is here murky and hesitant, she
drank espresso after bitter espresso

the base of her head flaming with small fires,
she waits for the grey air to lift its caution,
impatient for the window's slow morse

to time her shower,
hot water to hit her shoulder,
then she dressed for any type of weather

conscious as bees,
to the finest changes of sound,
and shadow, sweat and heat, she knows what she is to do

ossuary V

I must confess, I must, that early on
it was nothing to me, believe me,
you could dip your dingy hand in my chest

and it was nothing, I had enough bandages,
enough salves and enough razor blades,
I had a grin like jagged stone, like baleen plates

and then like sharks' teeth serrated, oblique,
hairs would tear you apart brushing against me,
but all the shifting wore me down, the efferent blood

petitions, I gave here, I gave there, I allowed,
of course here's my innocence, my shivering
never bothered me, much, I thought, it will pass

it will pass, but of course it didn't so here I am,
down to the last organ and happy to be there,
tired with it, exhausted to be there, bone dry

without walls, without embrasures, no height at all,
scatter bones, losing all relation to myself,
reified, common really, common the powdery skulls

the imponderable orbs in my forehead,
a lantern, around a light, what light,
the waxing crescent, the waning crescent come and go

unrelieved, along the coast, caustic sodas
stiffen the vertebrae rigid in the bristled winds,
blindness first, corroded lungs next

it was the same, the transparencies I thumbed,
for this for that, innumerable defences,
I drowned in vats of sulphurous defences

the crate of bones I've become, good
I was waiting to throw my limbs on the pile,
the mounds of disarticulated femurs and radii

but perhaps we were always lying there,
dead on our feet and recyclable,
toxic and imperishable, the ways to see us

I could hear music somewhere though, somewhere
in a distance backward or forward,
time split like willows

vague music that couldn't yet be music surely,
or was already music anyway,
it rushed ahead until it was a granule of light

the moon lay on the floor alone with us,
it drank the tiles,
it ate what we ate, it cupped our breath

the body skids where the light pools,
each bone has its lost dialect now,
untranslatable though I had so many languages

in the rooms above,
the hours spin their bangles,
supine, we listen

if I broke my chest open now,
with a small hammer,
I assure you, there would be nothing there

there would perhaps be a powder, a long thread,
a needle perhaps a photograph
of what I was to be to someone

I once saw "Lucia Monti" shine,
on the canvas of Jose Villegas Cordero,
in a museum, summing up

the black ages before her,
gleaming beyond
the aesthetic of sin and purgatory

will my bones glitter beyond these ages,
will they burn beyond the photographs'
crude economy

ossuary VI

this genealogy she's made by hand, this good silk lace,
Engels plaited to Bird, Claudia Jones edgestitched
to Monk, Rosa Luxemburg braids Coltrane

as far as she's concerned these names reshaped time
itself though time seems somehow set itself,
in time

in so few rooms that Yasmine herself is caught
and trapped in its coarse drenched net,
a blue crab angling and articulating

sideways, these names would help
here, but
such, such did not create the world or fix time

in that bulbous concentration,
of what matters,
what appears

Yasmine knows in her hardest heart,
that truth is worked and organized by some,
and she's on the wrong side always

she scrubs the tables till they're raw,
alive,
this she's done for three exact years

in this exact city,
whose exact location must remain vague,
here she is a polyglot, wise, too wise, silent like time

two hours before the onslaught of children,
their ferile enthusiasms,
the snow still falling over in Buffalo

that band of weather would not arrive
here,
before afternoon, before

what was the absence of weather,
and it always seems to be snowing in that city,
south of her exile, crouched as its name in winter fur

the children mattered, or so she told herself,
a platitude, people at base are craven,
more so children, their spongy senses

some days she spared them the sight of her,
the talk of her, except eat, sleep,
for fear of ruining them

where was she, that again, which city now,
which city's electric grids of currents,
which city's calculus of right and left angles

which city's tendons of streets, identical,
which city's domestic things,
newspapers, traffic, poverty

garbage collections, random murders,
shoplifting, hedge
cutting

all these coincidences,
the death of Robert Creeley, the bombing in Peshawar,
the habit of biting the lip

beginning to read *The Year of the Death
of Ricardo Reis*
for the twentieth time

and the light slow drizzle outside,
not to mention another ruin of all accords,
events happening in their order

a certain regularity,
which leads you to believe fancifully,
in coincidences

but which situate you at the apex of every
trajectory, composed irresolutely by you,
yet, only dimly recalled as consciously made by you

calculated, this flickering of light
in a specific meter of four four two,
the lone last light post on the street

the raised back of the stray cat,
at eleven every day,
resigned to hunger and random death

the same tiredness and stillness of the windy day,
when all the exercise instructions flew to the floor,
the day she decided to change places with Owusu

change chords, the four-note ending of her love,
slipped, dispassionate,
flared off, like Bird's exits

he had been right, how she'd become,
some receptacle for his spit, his sperm, his combed-out
hair, the shavings of his fingernails, each liquid phrase

he had uttered, she had drowned,
in the shell of her ear,
until his voice seemed to come from her

all because of attention to the wrong thing,
the still unknown-unknown she'd been, she'd pinned
her life to his existence when what she wanted was to be

at the crossing, when I am in the world,
she did not often think of that part of her life,
except of course

the way one remarks a low-grade fever,
a river that never recedes,
a chronic headache immune to narcotics

except it was always there,
struck, harder, the lack of self-forgiveness,
aluminium, metallic, artic, blinding

ossuary VII

venus, I could walk there on the ragged edge,
full of broken glass, ripped steel,
its ridge of bee stings

don't take me in from the window,
please,
don't remind me of my sweet voice

the water in my nostrils still,
the industry of birds, so busy,
in a hurry, hurry

going out in a stellar taxi,
querulous, smoking,
the year is two hundred and twenty-four days short

what force or will collected,
in that walking figure, erectus,
what fierce bright timbals

and which ambitious cells,
and which collisions of molecules,
reach their outer space sounding

don't take me in from the window, please,
I hear the crackle of the oceanic crust,
the fracture of extraterrestrial plains

I've got no time, no time, this epistrophe, no time,
wind's coming, no time,
one sunrise to the next is too long, no time

the heart lays cloaked and clawed,
its axial tilt jittery,
I'm using up all my light

all my light, don't pull me close,
in pools of pebbled water,
I hear thumbs plangent with string and air

I'm leaning out of my skull,
don't distract me,
I've never been here you know, you know

ossuary VIII

Havana, Yasmine arrived one early evening,
the stem of an orange dress,
a duffle bag, limp, with no possessions

the sea assaulted the city walls,
the air,
the birds assaulted the sea

she's not coastal,
more used to the interiors of northern cities,
not even their ancillary, tranquil green-black lakes

though nothing was ever tranquil about her,
being there out of her elemental America
unsettles her, untethers her

being alive, being human, its monotony
discomfited her anyway, the opaque nowness,
the awareness, at its primal core, of nothing

a temporary ache of safety,
leafed her back like unfurling fiddleheads,
she glimpsed below the obdurate seduction of Atlantic

and island shore,
when they landed, a contradiction,
a peppery drizzle, an afternoon's soft sun

the oiled air of Havana pushed its way onto the airplane,
leavened, domestic,
the Tupelov cabin like an oven darkening bread

she was alive in this place,
missing forever from her life in the other,
a moment's sentimentality could not find a deep home

what had been her life, what collection of events?
these then, the detonations,
the ones that led her to José Marti Airport

so first the language she would never quite learn,
though determined, where the word for her,
nevertheless, was *compañera*

and there she lived on rations of diction,
shortened syntax, the argot and tenses of babies,
she became allegorical, she lost metaphora, irony

in a small room so perfect she could paseo its rectangle,
in forty-four exact steps,
a room so redolent with brightness

cut in half by a fibrous bed,
made patient by the sometimish stove,
the reluctant taps, the smell of things filled with salt water

through the city's wrecked *avenidas*,
she would find the Malecón, the great sea wall
of lovers and thieves, jineteras and jineteros

and there the urban sea washed anxiety from her,
her suspicious nature found,
her leather-slippered foot against a coral niche

no avoiding the increment of observation here,
in small places small things get their notice,
not just her new sign language

oh yesterday, you were in a green skirt,
where's your smile today,
oh you were late to the corner on Tuesday

don't you remember we spoke at midday,
last week near the Coppelia,
you had your faraway handbag

your cigarette eyes,
your fine-toothed comb
for grooming peacocks, anise seeds in your mouth

you asked for a little lemon water,
you had wings in your hands,
you read me a few pages from your indelible books

what makes your eyes water so,
I almost drowned in them on Friday,
let me kiss your broken back, your tobacco lips

she recalled nothing of their encounters,
but why,
so brilliant at detail usually

the green skirt, the orange dress, the errant smile,
the middays all dissolved into
three, five, ten months in Havana

one night she walks fully clothed, like Bird,
into the oily pearl of the sea's surface,
coral and cartilage, bone and air, infrangible

and how she could walk straight out, her dress,
her bangles, her locking hair, soluble,
and how despite all she could not stay there

ossuary IX

what can I say about the storms,
the suns, the evenings, the moons
which have left the skies

the clouds' soft aggressions,
the seas leadening,
to brilliant slate

what is left of the winds' hoarse hands,
eclipsed by farms, the latitudes
hulahooped to the bottom of the stratospheres

the floors of oceans raked with backhoes,
the sea beds gutted,
the sheets of coral ripped by toenails of trawlers

the human skin translucent with diesel,
the lemon trees' inadvertent existences,
the satellite whales, GPS necklaces of dolphins and turtles

what can I say truly about the lungs alveoli
of plastic ornaments,
erupting, without oxygen

ossuary X

detonations, bullets,
there is the amber frisson of charged particles,
gravitational force so extravagant it is silence itself

the car ostentatiously broken down,
brown, wingless,
a wiry sweat down her backbone

Albany, snow outside, redundant,
two comrades glide, slip, slink toward
the bank's bronzed doors, they enter

then nothing, she is supposed to drive,
east of the bank there's a carwash,
an emaciated tree, a fire hydrant

he hums his coolness,
fills the car with himself, his sweet cigarettes,
then opens the door joint

she sees all the naive difficulty of their plan,
first the pathetic car under her gloved hands,
the tree, scabies on its bark, its obvious question mark

the winter hanging on, and hanging on,
its grubby sidewalks deserted,
the ramshackle street

"Cool," he says,
"Cool," she says,
"Power to the people." She. "Al hamdu lillaahi." He

he moves now, the same slinking gait,
as the two before,
the walk he'll use to disappear, later

as she, underground, will wait
for things to cool, though she confirms it to herself,
forever

for now he'll walk into the bank, for now
they are encircled by their beautiful predictions,
justice pumped through their veins, history will see

in the grizzled winter light,
she unlocks her finger from the steering wheel,
before he reaches the door she's at his shoulder

"I'll go, comrade." That last formality,
ground as though she'd quarried that sentence,
for the whole of their erogeny

this way she ends things and begins them,
a give in his muscles, as his assent,
"Power . . ." he begins, "to the people." She ends

you would think, you would think,
she felt fear,
none of them did

what was behind them was more fearsome,
than that ahead,
so no, no fear, what could that be today

a shelf of pigeons speculates,
first on the day,
then on the business below

the man halted in slippery stride,
the woman, gloved secretive hand on his shoulder,
they uncouple, the pigeons lose interest

the woman saunters under the puff of feathers,
the shelf shifts,
sets off a round of cooing and cuckling, resettling

the man turns to confront the reluctant car,
they must depend on its industry,
the lace of rotten rust that hangs on the doors

and fenders,
the open back windows that compensate
for the carburetor

the woman, she, Yasmine they call her,
her gloved right hand claws the metal at the bank's door,
her left nestles in her coat's reassuring pocket

it's over, one life, these two hands, this face
and what falls now,
the skies, the mornings, let them fall

the day, the withering in mirrors,
she cannot help but notice the years to come,
the door swings open

they are brilliant, those calendars spread out ahead,
and he might, or might not, be in them,
but she will

the small talon of her right hand sets to the massacre,
of her old life
its wingeing place, its spattering wavelengths

the cap of snow sky, the wedge
of fixed time that seals the body,
this new way she enters the bank, fatal

the door swings, cuts, her arm
rises to its lethal axis
"Don't anyone ..."

and nothing here defies her stillness,
not the morning commerce, the sandy scrape
of paper, the count of dollars, the surprise of tellers

the manager in the middle of his grey dominance,
nor the rickety guard who will betray his class
by putting up a fight

the planetary swivel of her head,
the comrades descending as angels to her goodness,
cicada swift, they echo her signal

the vault pried open from the manager's head,
the angels swoop into its vacuum,
swoop out to find the incidental guard

face crushed into gristle
by the butt of her avenging gyre,
they stop, newly awakened to her violence

it could be for anyone, them too, they know,
and quick too like living,
they show her their feathers and veins, open

and all retreat out the door,
past the prone, the urinated, the supine
to money, and now Yasmine

the hulk of brown rust shudders toward them,
the pigeons shuffle on the ledge,
garbage fattened through autumn for just this day

their beaks compacted into stone,
their feet the crud of tree bark,
they mind their own business, as they should

a drizzle of tiny ice pellets begins,
begins to fall,
the car coughs its reluctance, its indecisions

in vain, they tumble in, and without a word,
before the bank door erupts, or the supplicants of its
marble floor rise from their prayers, or sirens mewl

their syrup song,
they drive, drive, drive, drive, drive,
you would think it elegant the bucket of a rusted car

fleet, it understands occasion, urgency,
there might have been noise, there might not have been,
someone might have said something

or perhaps not,
it's all the same to her now,
that replete silence is what she heard

quiet they have, as, in some twilights,
and some mornings, that cool green
silence, like the one in books

and the one on days when you are home,
alone,
in rural houses, with fields or forests

the brown dragonfly, rusted wings,
flies along the highway out of town in long leaps,
it defies its cratered flanks, its overheated gasket

the earthbound metal of its thorax,
its compound eyes survey each angle of the flight,
for cops, patrols

ossuary XI

In the museum I sat with Jacob Lawrence's war,
his "victory," red and drenched, looked like defeat,
of course

he lifts these paintings from their ultraviolet vats,
from the Venusian winds that blow only west,
so much like him, or me, so much faster than our planet

such stillness, such stanzaic and raw elations,
when light appears on his paper,
he is already gone

I cried with him, held his lovely heads,
his angular gentle faces as my own, his bodies,
driven with intention, attack their catastrophe in gouache

"shipping out"
who could not see this like the passage's continuum,
the upsided down-ness, the cramp, the eyes compressed

to diamonds,
as if we could exhume ourselves from these mass graves,
of ships, newly dressed

if we could return through this war, any war,
as if it were we who needed redemption,
instead of this big world, our ossuary

so brightly clad, almost heroic, almost dead,
the celebratory waiting, the waiting,
the smell of wounds

the raw red compartments,
and the sharecropping, city-soothed
hands, big to kill something else

"another patrol" those three,
it could be any year then or now or in the future,
it could be home, dense clouds of carbon

and what border are they patrolling,
the thin diagonal between then and now,
and for whom their determination to mount

the fragile, fragile promise of humanity,
their painter knew the rimlessness of any hopes,
the limitless vicinities

which made all land perilous,
but patrol yes, of course for those who think
there's country to be gained

or any place that could be made safe,
the aeronautic spheres of raincoats,
the three valises, the chasm below them

prepared for any year, when will we arrive,
the steep gradient
of nothing

"beachhead" the arms wide as Olaudah Equiano,
the teeth fierce, bayonets for self-inflicted wounds,
suicides, and riots when the end of the day

is another precipice, another hill,
the imaginary line moving like revolving latitudes,
the heart then is an incendiary

the guitar strings of veins play a future
music still unheard, the bayonets
do their sacrificial work, close

that crucifix, that crucifix,
for those who believed,
it would take them to the other shore

by then, they were scarecrows
to the world, the wind whiffing through
ribs, the sound of air through paper and straw

though some element, iron perhaps or simply
the reflexive throws of a body losing
oxygen

beating out its last gushes,
of a living thing,
said, rest, place is somewhere

"going home" the wounds, hand, shoulder,
head, in gauze and blood,
fragile like eggs

an arm electrified and supplicant, spiked
with nuclear tips, its transmutation
in the verdant shoulder of penitentiaries

to come, who would mistake these wounds,
who call these declarations nothing,
these tender anatomies

love should meet them, nothing short,
these broken heads and propitiatory arms,
clean love should meet them

povertous dowries wait at the landings,
scapegoat necklaces ring harbours,
felonies of buses, and bars, and schools

and toilets, pocked laws will address
one hand, one foot, one ringlet of hair,
recant and harden, lapse, forget

this boat should remain out there,
will remain out here, ghosting in its watery solitude, praying
never to make shore

life rafts above and below the decks,
blue, blue as blue always anticipates
the football stadiums flooded, the defenceless hurricanes

"reported missing" again, missing again,
missing, again missing,
a body out of time, moving at a constant angle

its paths through space under these forces,
flights impossible to correct,
the unnecessary barbed wire's twisted crosses

horizontal and flimsy, these reports
reach no one,
satellites pick up eroded gigabits, in decades to come

perhaps but not now, cracked and crystalline,
this news lays on the soul's floor,
like numberless calendars

what does it matter, dates
by any reckoning dates don't count,
nor the sight of lilies that must bloom beyond the lines

to be missing in all hemispheres,
is a great feat for some, disappearances are not
uncommon, for the figure in the foreground

beyond this there must be oceans, there must be
telephones, there must be notebooks with data,
there might be the curve of snows and rains

the bends in roads, the horizons or the sunrises,
that is our hope behind this wire,
gravity must give up its hold on us

surely, gravity the jail guard, the commandante
of surfaces,
might relent someday, unpin us

surely it will unhook our hearts,
from us, anchorless we will scale our faithless
legs, shed jealous hours

someone will find us brittle-winged,
beyond the punishments of leaves, of docile trees,
of windows, of our own skeletons

someone, beyond the insatiable forecasts,
the small retinas, the heart's disease,
the tattered filaments

here we morph as twig and ice and bark
and butterfly, weed and spider, vespids,
hoping against predators

convergent mimesis, all means,
stand still and hope it passes, the diatonic,
ragged plumage of our disappearances

ossuary XII

one will leave at Corinth, one will make a way at Utica,
one at Syracuse, one split another highway,
she'll take Utica, deluged in a thousand years of silt

it doesn't exist anymore, she knows
its vertigo, its river sickness, its wars,
its sodden coordinates

37 degrees, 3 minutes, 28. 6 seconds,
North,
10 degrees, 3 minutes, 45.35 seconds East

and all its conquerors, up to the Vandals,
its last walls devoured by esparto
grass, and silt

she knows sulphur and iron and pumice stones,
what's buried near the house of treasures,
there's an archway there

and this is how she disappears, this is where,
into an ancient city, since no city here could offer
anything but brutal solitudes, ashen mirrors

fitting, phantom limbs, intermittent hearts,
they'll all return to start this epoch again,
catastrophes will swing their way

she'll take Utica, pawn her bangles,
her earrings, her school ring,
the gun, welded to her grip and furtive

no one mentions it, still hanging between them,
no one until she chooses Utica,
the man at the wheel, who doesn't know he cannot speak

her language anymore,
or touch her sisal robes, her skin, her votive throat,
the urn in her hand, which is a good urn for water

her new plan for the river's erosions where she is,
she knows what no one here will know
how in four millennia only one wall or two will survive

and so she will enter an earlier time,
contrive to change the river's course,
the forensic circumstances of her own

she's turned all directions in the car,
the one who leaves at Corinth will burrow,
become a diviner of aquifers

sniff sandstone and limestone where he's left, she'll
pass him in some market,
sometime. They'll know and not know each other

in Utica the day is different already by anticipation,
the cap of snow sky pried loose,
a stark white shaft of road declares itself here

there she answers, commands the car to stop,
the brakes embrace, the wretched muffler hacks,
helpless, the gas tank is exhausted anyway

the driver, dumbstruck for once,
she is leaving, will leave it to her angels to explain,
she will float out on the winter's breath

two months from now, one dares to say, maybe more,
at the safe place, we'll meet,
now she laughs without leaving, short, deep leaves

safe place, she laughs, safe,
safe place, she is in stitches, the Syracuse teenager
giggles. You're righteous, Yas, stoned righteous

she takes to leave, the man they all consign
to Corinth begs through their hysteria,
but what was I here, what

and is this far enough away, a far enough way,
or are we still slaves in this old city,
back then, back then, always back then

drive, man, I'm sick of back then,
fucking straitjacket, man,
then and still now, get me to another country

another time when time isn't measured
like now, look, man, this ain't for me,
let's go on, find another world, find some elevation, cool?

this is our bed, the driver says, the first time he says
anything, since all events that rearranged
their lives occurred, since the axis of the day

regraphed his authority, and snow outside
took root in all their hearts against him,
this is our bed, he said it like it was inevitable

like it was some sour juice, some medicine,
they had to take and admit,
or the second vertebra of the neck, the pivot

now they know how hopeless he is,
now they hear what once seemed like courage,
what once hung out of his mouth, like his swagger

they'd envied in hallways when they were frightened,
his languor and that added ingredient of daring,
those outrageous shoes and hats

his time in the penitentiary,
when he'd read Marx and Lenin
and took the nickname Trotsky, from a brother

how he said once he was tired of seeing his mother's
heart broken, no word that he was the one who broke it,
she could have handled all the ache of America, save him

and a gun exposed, the faults he laid in all their plans,
not wilful but like this bed talk,
careless, or heading to some unexpected doom

and then this rattled ride from one old town,
to another, the bald tires skidding
on these hard diamonds of ice, the passing worlds

of forest and farm deserted now like their lives,
though perhaps not, their lives were always deserted,
always factional in the soul, always divided

so against themselves, their cells split,
their laughters bleached, blanched,
and this is what they were trying to lose, or gain

and now he'd said, this is our bed,
not mine, says Yas, not yours either, she
tells the man from Corinth, not yours

raze Corinth, every pot, every ugly thing,
make alphabets extinct,
there's the silence that is to come for her

her gun leans in his chest,
its letter O burns as if he's shot,
and she might as well, he thinks, his life will sink

anyway, phyllite fathoms
we'll never meet again he says, missing
her fire, her new violence, her charm

the way she is vapour already,
hot dances, a steel mallet, a stone axe,
he sees her wet feet, meteoric heart

what was I here, he asks her,
she, he should have followed, known her,
rather than the avatar with his hands on the winter road

everything to me more everything than most,
he can feel his face on icy decades to come,
this small damp town, this bald meridian of his life

sedimentary, limestone, dolostone,
tell me again I was something to you,
tell me, so afraid he would fade away from this new Yas

in shale, having never known her,
the car is full of all their last possibilities,
all the spherical tumult of former fears return

the ones in childhood tenements,
in gazes through low hallways,
food smells, in their oily jackets

the ever-peeling walls, the idiosyncratic
hobbies of eating chalk, kicking doorstops,
bouncing balls, of every circumference

and here no dreaming except to jump off,
rooftops, fall twelve or twenty storeys,
to the pavement below, intact

to observe some rites of Sunday churches,
or more radically Saturdays with straight-backed
mothers, their arms like ramparts spiked

to hold back the inevitable concrete storms,
of waste
and drift

too much for them this job of catching air,
with butterfly nets,
of stopping water with bottomless jars

too much collecting the sloughed skins
of this world's eyelids,
too much shattering the squares of caged fingers

it's a wonder they don't burst open on the road,
here the mildewed roof of the car is the sky,
here their bones erupt like skeleton over skeleton

and going on seems like their curse,
until they hear the inevitable sirens in the dull foggy
distances, behind them, they turn

the hoary road rolls away, the one who will leave
at Syracuse, his chin feathered in nineteen-year-old down,
he is afraid of nothing

not troopers, not dogs, not bullets, not knives,
not jail, already most of his short life has been
enclosure, institutions, so what, he thinks

he'll take the vacant road, he'll take it on foot,
if he has to, bare foot
he loves the fog closing in, the clouds shutting the sky

the day, like every day for him, an emergency not a life,
he grins with tension, bitter dog, he says,
I could use some bitter dog, some reefer too, good reefer

they suddenly see their wounds in him,
the gashes in their skins, the gouging, scraping
places left, open raw cavities of their long, long losses

history will enter here, whistling like train wheels,
boat winches,
the road will either end or won't, the cops catch up or not

they will arrive wherever,
they will be at war with their veins,
at war with all accounts, at war, so what

and, look, anyway, they're all composed in bony anchors
at the feet, they'll escape or they won't,
those are eternal cops behind them, glacial and planetary

yeah, Yas repeats, some bitter dog,
they laugh for him, that laugh, so prodigious,
the car's got endless fuel, they drive on

ossuary XIII

if only I had something to tell you, from here,
some good thing that would weather
the atmospheres of the last thirty years

I would put it in an envelope,
send it to my past life,
where someone would open it and warn the world

though, this news would arrive corroded,
you would still read it, its rust blooding,
its oxygen asperous and brittle

I'd hope you would still understand it
from here, what and how, I've been wasted,
these metal glyphs, falling and then

as if I'm gone, fingernails
peeled back in salt,
what it is, to lie down in water each night

to feel the mouth full like drowning,
the lungs like pinned butterflies,
and then as if the heart was eaten out, cored

this would do you no good to hear,
that from one January to the next,
nothing happened much that was not the same

arteries of stone,
capillaries of desolate cement,
and no kisses

rather I should say nothing, leave you to it,
make your own vain flights,
see how it goes, I can't tell time anyway

what is the sense then in sending this envelope,
porous as it is, don't worry,
look out, that's all it will say, but go on

go on, the brilliant future doesn't wait,
forget this,
I've been wasted, look, the chest like a torn bodice

ripped the guts right out of me, go,
go, my toes are eaten away by frost and rubber,
some chemical has boiled my eyes

the rest of me's been stolen,
I should say wrecked, well let's say,
I never knew it, like wire

full of jealousies, red coils,
like swallowing powder above everything,
the throat of broken glass and thorny sprigs

the falling slabs of skies in each deluged year,
I'd like to know how my assassination took place,
only why go over the summer

it was whatever it was,
one day a certain breeze, a certain
humidity, a fan of spirea waving

the sure thought that life would not be lived
here, like other people, a sickness
of uncertainties, of shifts

how to say I wish for permanence,
then I cast it off as dullness, stupidity,
then wish again for certainty, to be

in life, sitting at a bar,
cigars hanging from my fingers, I'd tip
the waitress half the cost of everything

to inhabit whole,
which is to exist simply, the bone
is an organ like any other

this was the chance, but everything can
be discussed, except that we are predatory
so on we go, take no note of what's been said here

the presumptive cruelties,
the villages that nursed these since time,
it's always in the lyric

the harsh fast threatening gobble,
the clipped sharp knifing, it's always,
in the lyric

and how I'm never left to take the sun,
to take my ease, or sleep
in the transparent parts of the day

but I'm one of the ones who likes to think,
of humankind,
I read that one can be morally exhausted

what fool said that,
what enemy of conscience,
after all this time, I'm naive as wrinkled babies

it may be useless now, to say
the awkward life, the hovering life, the
knowing life, born so early in me

known so deeply, the palm,
the sepal, unopened,
the calyx knotted, and what couldn't matter

now that we are speeding on
our atrocious axis,
the lost streets, the crashed doorsteps

the so much sorrow that cracks eyes,
such perpetual belittlings,
a woman is lying sideways on her arms

a grandfather is drifting,
into the roadway again,
a hoarse laugh outside the windows

cosmic orange flowers are waving
in their distance, what of
the patent-leather shoes hanging

from legs near the ice-cream bench,
what species of ants live in sugary maple trees
that are about to die in a former year

who will see the bedraggled gawping doorways,
the solitary deaths of finches that winters strand,
before smiles were wire, and before knives

were food and teeth were asphalt,
before sunlight was acid, on cedar porches
and hair was exiled beneath gas stoves,

the shawls strewn everywhere, sightless
walks in cities, the bony sands, the acidic
shorelines of skyscrapers, the seething airwaves all over

the starving boats and lithic frigates,
stingless bees, the canvas shirts,
the bright darkness, the clotted riverbeds

the flaking skins, the second thoughts,
the afterthoughts, dry timbre of air pockets,
the inabilities to live, the inabilities to live

right or fully, not live right,
the liveried skin, the flesh thickened with cancers,
tumours of sightlines, readjusted

ankles, fenced mouths,
mechanic vulva, plastic toenails,
pincered knee, nib of palms, wire
lifelines, elongated radius, cellular

disintegration, *dedos destruidos*
swollen tongues, *espalda goteando*,
snowy pubis, stone aorta

leathered skin, gelatinous skin,
threnodic skin, shrugged hands, you see,
I've sat here all this time being reasonable

like this, in the eye-filled years, the wall-filled years,
the returning years, the formaldehyde years,
the taxidermy years, the dishevelled years

the years of viola and mahalia and tamasine,
and gangadia and white shirts,
and sightlessness, flatsight, only sight

and coarseness,
leapy calves, leaden breath, sodden
leaden sicklyness, baked songs

I've prolonged skin bits, powdered, ashed
notebooks, copybooks,
nicks of hearts, cardboard spleen

runny veins,
husks of knuckles, the eclogite tibias,
some parts that went missing, April 19

if only someone opens this in that year,
I hope they won't understand all of it,
it should be dust too, it will, it will

look for nothing it will say, the cataclasite sacral crest,
the gutted thorax, except the schistic rib cages,
the feldspar wrists, the hyoid bone, what's left

the prosthetic self and all the broken bodies,
collapsed chest caves, will appear dressed, clattering
down streets, in all fashions of all years,

no one suspected the inventions,
I felt my own acid hand on the knee joints,
some gritty fluid on the mandible, the letter-writing finger

ossuary XIV

not until April did she make her way,
across the Niagara River,
the drop from rail to water, decisive and honest

the train, trolling the back of gluttonous
small cities,
dead vehicles slackly gathered, heaped

rickety and disorderly, to watch her,
spectacle, sheathed in a guiltless dress,
a new passport, a razor-bladed photo

the woman died in a car accident, she was
Caucasian, but the forger's razor blade fixed that,
and the year she died, six and counting

and the state, way south, and the family,
all perished too, all concentrated now
in Yasmine, in the train's window pane

rattle, piled truck dross, old bus carcasses,
ripped plastic with sonar senses passed,
then the ice-sweet grapevines greeted her

apple trees, collecting their bare bones
for another bearing,
and acres of desultory brick houses

gearing up for quixotic summers,
cemeteries, their solitary collections of meagre
stone biographies go by, lumber in waiting

bales, frightful garbage,
but the sky, the sky,
air glass, lung-widening sky

if she could remain suspended
between that steel, that river's gush,
this bridge, this brief relief

the only thing that amazes her now is the earth,
its ubiquitous snows and lights,
and waters, its combustible air, its nocturnal

screeches and beeps, its miraculous
colours,
what to say about that, everything

that hasn't been said, no names
for those, only ineffective attempts,
but the eyes know better, know this failure

not before April, not before joints disentangled,
their instinctual fears, could she get clear,
of a grey translucent feeling, to trust the forger

take the train toward the river's bridge,
toward the electric fields the diagonal bungalows,
graveyards of car tires, and still vines, marsh

keeps struggling up, waste like costal cartilage,
bandages the limbs of sumach, underwears the shoots,
ropes their feet, she's tired of struggling up

too, along the train's ridged centipedal back,
the spring sweats, the wind snaps
insects in two, the deserted

willows lean, inhale the tentative air
of this April,
supine, cunning month, or perhaps

fickle, or perhaps out of control,
or perhaps this damp new month will
share out its thirty days, in its usual rain

and gasps of sunlight,
and occasional blisters of snow,
its incipient lilac, her new-washed intentions

to be someone else, to be, that infinitive
that, for instance, set her on this train,
she talked to no one, found and kept a lone seat

her legs like a gate, her chin
steady on its elegiac stem, and that hand,
its history spread like spider orchids across her lap

what did this arriving city know of her,
her recumbent violence, her real
name like a music, with perfume on the end

Yasmine, some long-fingered horn player,
could blow confessions over those two cool syllables,
she'd take the teeth grit of the brusking train wheels

a wheeling bird outside, an anonymous bird,
call it oriole, call it flycatcher, more than likely,
seemed to follow her window for a while

she slept head bobbing on that alert filament,
and somehow six or so other passengers know,
to stay away, stay clear from the woman in her rookery

the woman whom the bird outside was following,
call it crow, call it hawk, call it peregrine falcon,
call her brooding even in sleep

it left when she woke up fully, call it
magpie then, her eyes its diamond, its brilliant metal,
call it heron, great blue, long-legged migrating alone

north, it broke off, it took air,
flew into an apostrophe,
heading to the wet marsh of another lake

Yasmine gathers her legs, her perfunctory luggage,
scythes the train car with her lethal gait,
stands first at the door when the wheels stop

she steps into another country, another
constellation of bodies,
her compass reset to what reckonings

at the Maple Leaf farms, Yasmine signs
to get in, signs to get out,
this is not a nuclear installation but a killing farm

for chickens,
she lines up, as each woman does,
on a steel plank, each woman with a knife

to dissect, as each woman knows how,
viscera, fat, muscle, tendon,
this daily killing, daily flesh eating

water dripping from the tables,
waterlogged to their feet, arthritic and cold,
to cut a particular part out

each woman knows what part,
their hands,
are deadly

ossuary XV

they ask sometimes, who could have lived,
each day,
who could have lived each day knowing

some massacre was underway, some repression,
why, anyone, anyone could live this way,
I do, I do

anyone, I'm not unique, not shy,
someone goes out for milk and butter,
and returns with gashed face, wrung larynx

practically ancient,
I'm not fooling myself, I've tried,
this regime takes us to the stone pit every day

we live like this,
each dawn we wake up, our limbs paralyzed,
shake our bones out, deliver ourselves

to the sharp instruments for butchering,
to appease which rain god,
which government god, which engine god

I don't know,
I know the abattoirs for carving, the everyday chemical
washes, and the fissile air in any regular sky

so here we lie in our bare arms,
here the ribs for a good basket, a cage,
the imperishable mandible, the rhetorical metatarsals

the hip's alertness, the skull's electricity
firing, the lit cigarette tip of the backbone
leans for its toxic caresses

here we lie in folds, collected stones
in the museum of spectacles,
our limbs displayed, fract and soluble

were this a painting, it would combust canvases,
this lunate pebble, this splintered phalanx,
I can hardly hold their sincere explosions

ACKNOWLEDGEMENTS

The following works were instrumental during the writing
of this poem.

Theory: *The Eighteenth Brumaire of Louis Bonaparte* by Karl
Marx; *The Origin of the Family, Private Property, and the State*
by Friedrich Engels; *Endless Forms Most Beautiful* and *The
Making of the Fittest* by Sean B. Carroll; *Human Zoos*, eds. Pascal
Blanchard, Nicolas Bancel et al.; *Everyone Talks About the
Weather . . . We Don't: The Writings of Ulrike Meinhoff*, ed. Karin
Baur, preface by Elfriede Jelinek; and *Long Time Gone* by
William Lee Brent.

Music: "Epistrophy" by Thelonious Monk; "Ornithology"
by Charles "Bird" Parker, Jr.; "Venus" by John Coltrane; and
"Pithecanthropus Erectus" by Charles Mingus.

Paintings: *War Series* by Jacob Lawrence and *Lucia Monti* by
Jorge Villegas Cordero.

Don McKay for the hike in Banff.

Thanks to Ellen Seligman and Anita Chong for their
patience, Heather Sangster once again for her commas.